Dick Bruna

Snuffy's Puppies

Methuen Children's Books

Snuffy is a little brown dog.

One day she is so quiet and still,

her mistress thinks something is wrong.

"What is it, Snuffy?

We'll take you to the vet.

He will know what the matter is."

The vet smiles.

"Snuffy is very well.

Soon she will have some puppies."

Everyone is very glad.

Snuffy is very hungry.

She has extra food,

to help her stay

strong and healthy.

Nine weeks later,

in the middle of the night,

what do you think happens?

Turn the page and see.

Three little brown puppies

are born. They are so new,

their eyes have not opened.

But they are hungry already.

Snuffy lies on her side

to let her babies feed.

Soon they can walk

a little bit. But sometimes

they bump and fall down.

Their eyes are still closed.

When they are three weeks old,

they can open their eyes and see.

Now they are ready to play.

Snuffy has a lot to teach them.

The little pups learn

to go outside for certain things!

The puppies have their own dishes

just like their mother's.

They always lick their dishes clean,

and grow bigger every day.

Snuffy likes to watch her

little family. She thinks,

what fine puppies I have,

the best ones in the world.

BRUNA BOOKS

The little bird
Tilly and Tessa
The fish
The egg
Circus
The king
The sailor
The school
The apple
Pussy Nell
Snuffy
Snuffy and the fire
A story to tell
Another story to tell
I am a clown
My vest is white
I can count
I can count more
I can read
I can read more
I can read difficult words
I can dress myself
Through the Year
  with Boris Bear

Miffy
Miffy's birthday
Miffy at the seaside
Miffy in the snow
Miffy at the zoo
Miffy goes flying
Miffy in hospital
Miffy at the playground
Miffy's dream
Miffy's bicycle
Miffy at school
Poppy Pig
Poppy Pig's Garden
Poppy Pig goes to Market
Poppy Pig's Birthday
When I'm big
I know about numbers
I know more about numbers
I know about shapes
I can make music
Farmer John
The lifeboat
Find my Hat
Back to Front
My Sport Book

ALSO BY DICK BRUNA

Dick Bruna's ABC Frieze
Dick Bruna's 123 Frieze
Dick Bruna's Animal Frieze
Dick Bruna's Nature Frieze
Dick Bruna's Read-with-Miffy Frieze
The Christmas Book
B is for Bear
Blue Boat
Dick Bruna's Animal Book
Dick Bruna's Word Book
Bruna Zig Zags
  My House
  Playing in Winter
  My Playtime
  My Street
  My Garden
  My Animals
Bruna Board Books
  Good Morning
  Good Night
Dick Bruna Postcards

First published in Great Britain 1987
by Methuen Children's Books Ltd,
11 New Fetter Lane, London EC4P 4EE
Exclusively arranged and produced by
Mercis publishing bv., Amsterdam
Text copyright © Dick Bruna 1986
English translation copyright © 1987
Methuen Children's Books
Illustrations Dick Bruna, © copyright Mercis bv. 1986
Printed and bound by Brepols Fabrieken NV, Turnhout, Belgium
ISBN 0 416 05072 7